PAST and PRESENT

No 39

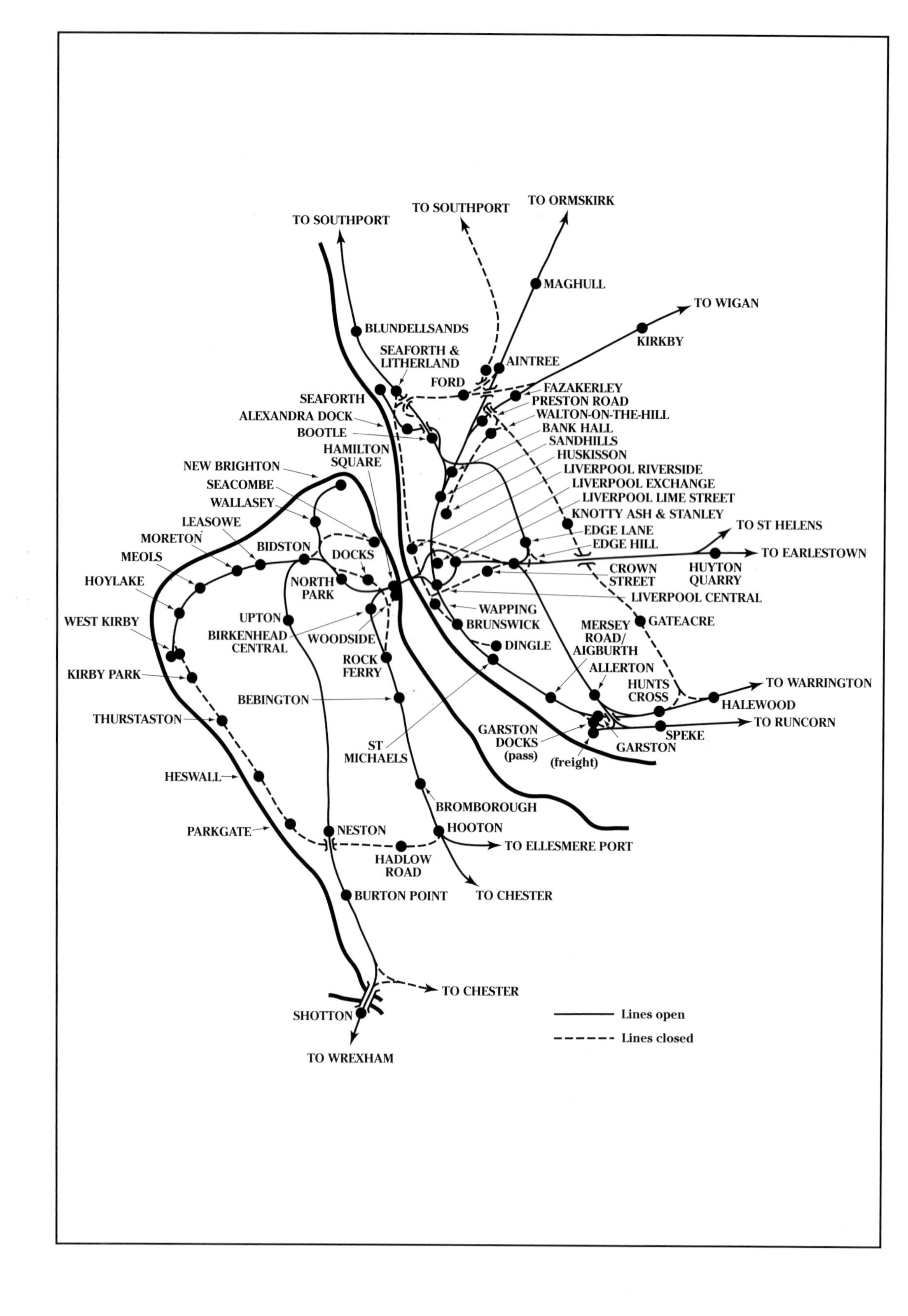
TO SOUTHPORT
TO SOUTHPORT
TO ORMSKIRK
MAGHULL
TO WIGAN
KIRKBY
BLUNDELLSANDS
SEAFORTH &
LITHERLAND
AINTREE
FORD
FAZAKERLEY
PRESTON ROAD
WALTON-ON-THE-HILL
SEAFORTH
ALEXANDRA DOCK
BOOTLE
BANK HALL
SANDHILLS
HAMILTON
SQUARE
HUSKISSON
NEW BRIGHTON
LIVERPOOL RIVERSIDE
SEACOMBE
LIVERPOOL EXCHANGE
WALLASEY
LIVERPOOL LIME STREET
KNOTTY ASH & STANLEY
LEASOWE
TO ST HELENS
EDGE LANE
MORETON
BIDSTON
EDGE HILL
TO EARLESTOWN
MEOLS
DOCKS
HUYTON
QUARRY
CROWN
STREET
HOYLAKE
NORTH
PARK
LIVERPOOL CENTRAL
WAPPING
UPTON
WEST KIRBY
GATEACRE
BRUNSWICK
MERSEY
ROAD/
AIGBURTH
BIRKENHEAD
CENTRAL
WOODSIDE
DINGLE
ROCK
FERRY
ALLERTON
KIRBY PARK
TO WARRINGTON
HUNTS
CROSS
HALEWOOD
BEBINGTON
THURSTASTON
TO RUNCORN
SPEKE
GARSTON
DOCKS
(pass)
GARSTON
ST
MICHAELS
(freight)
HESWALL
BROMBOROUGH
PARKGATE
NESTON
HOOTON
TO ELLESMERE PORT
HADLOW
ROAD
BURTON POINT
TO CHESTER
TO CHESTER
SHOTTON
TO WREXHAM
Lines open
Lines closed

BRITISH RAILWAYS

PAST and PRESENT

No 39

Liverpool and Wirral

Paul Shannon & John Hillmer

Past and Present

Past & Present Publishing Ltd

First published in 2002

British Library Cataloguing in Publication Data

A catalogue record for this book is available from the British Library.

ISBN 1 85895 199 2

Past & Present Publishing Ltd
The Trundle
Ringstead Road
Great Addington
Kettering
Northants NN14 4BW

Tel/Fax: 01536 330588
email: sales@nostalgiacollection.com
Website: www.nostalgiacollection.com

Printed and bound in Great Britain

HAMILTON SQUARE, BIRKENHEAD: Opened in 1886, Hamilton Square was the first Mersey Railway station on the Cheshire side of the river, situated close to the centre of Birkenhead. The entrance to the station is pictured on 20 April 1954, with an advertisement for the frequent service through the tunnel to Liverpool, taking just 3 minutes. A Victorian post-box can be seen to the left of the rear open-platformed Birkenhead Corporation double-decker bus, on route 22, heading for Woodside.

In the 'present' picture of 9 January 2002 a new sign (illuminated at night) has been added to the near side of the tower, a modern building has been constructed to the left, and a number of other buildings, including the industrial chimney beyond the traffic lights, have been demolished. *H. C. Casserley/JCH*

CONTENTS

HAMILTON SQUARE
STATION
FREQUENT ELECTRIC TRAINS
R731 HWA

LIVERPOOL LIME STREET: In the BR era Lime Street consolidated its position as Liverpool's principal main-line station, with regular expresses to London Euston complemented by other long-distance services to destinations such as Newcastle, Hull and Plymouth. The West Coast Main Line electrification scheme reached Lime Street in January 1962, although it was several more years before electric trains could run all the way to London. Even then the majority of trains remained steam- or diesel-worked, as there were no plans to electrify in the Manchester or Wigan directions. On 19 September 1961 rebuilt 'Royal Scot' 4-6-0 No 46119 *Lancashire Fusilier* waits to depart with the 11.00am to Newcastle.

The track and platform layout at Lime Street has changed little in the last 40 years. Most trains these days are in the hands of various types of diesel unit, with the use of locomotives restricted to Virgin services on the West Coast Main Line. 'Pacer' unit No 142060 departs from platform 3 with the 1435 local to Wigan North Western on 15 February 2002. *Michael Mensing/PDS*

INTRODUCTION

Between 1830, when the Liverpool & Manchester Railway made its historic début, and 1874, when the Cheshire Lines Committee opened its approach from Garston to Liverpool Central, the railways of Liverpool grew from nothing to a well-developed network of interconnected lines. The natural geography of Liverpool – the fact that it is built on a large outcrop of sandstone – gave its railway network two distinctive features: one was the relatively large number of tunnels on the approach to the city's passenger and freight termini, and the other was the concentration of most radial routes on broadly north-south alignments parallel to the Mersey estuary. The growing importance of Liverpool docks also encouraged the routing of railways along the estuary, as the various companies vied to increase their share of the maritime traffic.

Until the Grouping of 1923, the main-line railways of Liverpool were essentially divided between three companies: the London & North Western Railway (LNWR), the Lancashire & Yorkshire Railway (L&Y) and the Cheshire Lines Committee (CLC). The busiest system was that of the LNWR, with Lime Street becoming the terminus for prestige London expresses as well as a whole range of long-distance and local services. The LNWR also built its own access route from Edge Hill to the north end of Liverpool Docks, used mainly by freight but providing a link for passenger trains between Lime Street and the Southport line.

The L&Y system was characterised by one of the first electrification schemes in Great Britain, which saw the busy local lines to Southport and Ormskirk equipped with conductor rails in the early 1900s. By this time the city had already benefited from another pioneering feat of engineering – the construction of the all-electric Liverpool Overhead Railway (LOR) between Seaforth and Dingle. The two electrified systems met at Seaforth & Litherland station, but were never fully integrated.

The CLC was a relatively late arrival in central Liverpool, but it gained an important share of the passenger business between Liverpool and Manchester as well as local traffic to and from places such as Garston and Gateacre. It also tapped into the lucrative docks traffic by means of connections at Brunswick in the south and Huskisson in the north.

The first half of the 20th century brought few major changes to Liverpool's railways. The first significant passenger closures were the LNWR Garston Dock branch in 1947 and local services between Edge Hill and Alexandra Dock in 1948. Regular services between Gateacre and Aintree and between Gladstone Dock and Kirkby were withdrawn in the early 1950s, while the LOR ceased operations in the same decade.
Had the Beeching Report been fully implemented, further closures would have followed in the 1960s, including – incredibly – the Liverpool to Southport line. Fortunately, that threat was averted, and the worst that happened to Liverpool was the concentration of its main-line services on Lime Street, leaving Central and Exchange stations with only a limited future. On the positive side, Lime Street was included in the West Coast Main Line 25kV AC electrification scheme, and new diesel units brought a new lease of life to non-electrified local services.

The 1970s saw some cutbacks in the freight network, with docks traffic declining sharply and the wagonload business severely curtailed. But the opening of Seaforth container terminal brought a welcome revival, and the area around Garston and Speke continued to produce large freight volumes. As for passengers, the 1970s was a decade of major expansion, with the opening of the Loop and Link lines under Liverpool city centre and the electrification of routes to Kirkby and Hunts Cross. Investment in railway infrastructure on that scale is unlikely to come to Merseyside again.

At the start of the 21st century the railway system in Liverpool appears stable, with no major threats to the present network, but little prospect of substantial expansion. As with the British railway network as a whole, the greatest uncertainty lies with freight. The ambitious aspirations of EWS in the late 1990s have quietly been forgotten, and the emphasis is now on stemming the loss of existing rail traffic to road. The Strategic Rail Authority has, however, proposed one significant investment scheme for Liverpool: the re-opening the chord at Olive Mount Junction. This would allow access to Liverpool Docks without reversing, leading to improvements in journey times and reliability.

Inevitably in a book such as this, many of the scenes present a rather depressing picture of Liverpool's railways. Many former station sites are now unrecognisable beneath redevelopment, or are in the process of returning to nature. Freight is concentrated on just a handful of locations. But there are also some positive tales to tell. The comparison at Brunswick is between a disused line with no station in the 1970s and a busy commuter line with a new station in 2002. Two of the pictures in Liverpool docks illustrate the freight revival that has taken place gradually over the last 20 years. Clearly, railways continue to play an important role in Liverpool's economy.

Although Birkenhead and Liverpool are separated by the River Mersey, the close ties between them go back many years. A ferry was associated with the Benedictine monks on the Cheshire side from 1330, when Birkenhead was the larger of the two settlements. The first railway on the Wirral was opened in 1840 by the Chester & Birkenhead Railway (later to become the Birkenhead Railway Joint Committee operated by the GWR and LNWR). This was followed by several quite distinct lines. In 1866 the Joint Committee opened a branch from Hooton to Parkgate, subsequently extended in 1886 to its own terminus station at West Kirby. Also in 1866, the Wirral Railway opened a line from Birkenhead Docks (later re-named Birkenhead North) to Hoylake. Due to lack of traffic that line closed in 1870, but it was re-opened two years later by the Hoylake & Birkenhead Rail & Tramway Company (later to be known as the Wirral Railway) and extended in 1878 to West Kirby. In the same year Woodside terminus opened as a replacement for Monks Ferry in Birkenhead.

The next route to open was the Mersey Railway line under the river from Green Lane (Birkenhead) to Liverpool in 1886, creating the first competition to the ferries. The branch to Birkenhead Park followed in 1888, making the crucial connection with the Wirral Railway. Of equal importance three years later was the extension south from Green Lane to Rock Ferry, enabling passengers from Chester to change at Rock Ferry for a direct service to Liverpool. The branch to Wallasey and New Brighton opened also in 1888 and that to Seacombe in 1895. The final piece of major infrastructure followed a year later when the North Wales & Liverpool Railway line opened from Hawarden Bridge to Bidston, where it connected with the Wirral Railway, again offering an interchange to Liverpool.

On the Mersey Railway there had been constant problems with steam locomotives hauling passenger trains through the river tunnel, due to the gradients and smoke – despite the locos being fitted with steam condensers. Although in a poor financial state, the Mersey Railway concluded a deal with Westinghouse to electrify the system as a 'showcase'. In the early hours of 3 May 1903 the last steam-hauled train ran through the tunnel and the same morning electric trains came into passenger service. It was not until 1938 that the lines from Birkenhead Park to West Kirby and New Brighton were electrified, and it took a further 47 years for the third rail to continue on from Rock Ferry to Hooton, eventually reaching Chester in 1993 and to Ellesmere Port the following year.

Competition from the car and bus brought about the conclusion of passenger services on the West Kirby to Hooton branch in 1956 and complete closure in 1962. The short branch to Seacombe had already succumbed in 1960. Through take-overs and mergers over the years, three of the 'Big Four' (LMS, GWR and LNER) were active on the Wirral until brought together through Nationalisation in 1948. British Rail did not quite last 50 years as Privatisation brought major change. Merseyrail Electrics Ltd was set up as a free-standing unit, and a successful tender for the franchise came from MTL Trust Holdings, which took effect from 19 January 1997. In February 2000 Arriva plc purchased MTL and initially agreed to continue with the franchise for one year, later renegotiated to expire in February 2003. It was re-named Arriva Trains Merseyside Ltd 2001. An exception was the Bidston-Wrexham line, which is a First North Western route at the time of writing, but may well be absorbed by the Wales & Borders train operating company.

Freight played an important part in the development of Birkenhead's railway system. By 1857 over 200,000 tons of coal passed through Birkenhead docks, and in 1885 there were 170 coal trains arriving per week. The town became an important flour-milling centre by 1860, which created considerable inward grain traffic. At the turn of the century meat and cattle had also become extremely important, and five or six meat trains left each day. By 1920 the Mersey Dock & Harbour Company had 48 miles of track throughout the docks system. Birkenhead continued to be the principal port for importing meat even until the 1950s, when the cattle traffic still required 150-200 wagons a day.

Tonnages of freight started to decline after the Second World War, and by 1973 shipment traffic to the South and North docks had ceased. In 1980 the imported iron ore traffic from Bidston Dock finished, following the end of steel-making at Shotton. Miscellaneous wagonload traffic, including grain and steel, fizzled out in the 1980s, leaving just the coal concentration depot to linger until 1993. After that, sidings were removed and the line through the docks quickly became overgrown. In the last few years there have been rumours of a possible freight revival at Birkenhead, but, as so often with freight proposals, there are many hurdles to be overcome and no firm agreement has been reached at the time of writing.

Finally, we must record our thanks to the many photographers and holders of photographic collections who made their archive material available to us. We are especially grateful to Bryan Wilson and the late Jim Peden for supplying caption information and for helping us to locate some of the 'past' views.

John Hillmer, Wilmslow
Paul Shannon, Chester

BIBLIOGRAPHY

ABC Railway Freight Operations *by Paul Shannon* (Ian Allan)
The Birkenhead Railway (LMS & GW Joint) *by T. B. Maund* (RCTS)
BR Steam Motive Power Depots: LMR *by Paul Bolger* (Ian Allan)
BR Track Diagrams: No 4 London Midland Region (Quail Map Co)
The Directory of British Engine Sheds (Part 2) *by Griffiths & Smith* (OPC)
The Directory of Railway Stations *by R. V. J. Butt* (Patrick Stephens)
The Handbook of Steam Motive Power Depots (3) *by Paul Smith* (Platform 5)
Liverpool Overhead Railway 1893-1956 (National Museums and Galleries on Merseyside and the University of Liverpool)
Merseyrail Electrics: The Inside Story *by T. B. Maund* (NBC Books)
Merseyside & District Railway Stations *by Paul Bolger* (The Bluecoat Press)
Railway Stations of Wirral *by the Merseyside Railway History Group* (Ian & Marilyn Boumphrey)
A Regional History of the Railways of Great Britain: Volume 10 The North West *by Geoffrey O. Holt* (David & Charles)
Regional Railway Centres: North West *by Rex Christiansen* (Ian Allan)
Shed Side on Merseyside *by Kenn Pearce* (Sutton Publishing)
Walking, Cycling & Riding along the Wirral Way (Ian & Marilyn Boumphrey)

Back issues of:
Branch Line News
The Railway Observer
The Railway Magazine
Railway World
Modern Railways
Rail

EXCHANGE STATION
MERCURY COURT
P293 PRJ

The Lancashire & Yorkshire Railway

LIVERPOOL EXCHANGE: The Lancashire & Yorkshire Railway (L&Y) and the East Lancashire Railway jointly opened their Tithebarn Street terminus on what became the site of Exchange station in 1850. That facility soon became inadequate for the L&Y's rapidly expanding range of long-distance and suburban train services and, during the 1880s, it was completely rebuilt, with ten platforms instead of five and with the extra provision of a luxury hotel. The station name was changed to Exchange in 1886. Third-rail electrification was completed as early as 1904; however, this was only ever intended for suburban trains and for the next 60 years steam traction prevailed on long-distance workings. The photograph shows Class 5 4-6-0 No 45330 awaiting departure from Exchange in March 1967. This was just 17 months before the end of standard gauge steam on British Railways; Exchange was to have the distinction of receiving BR's last scheduled steam-hauled passenger train, the 2125 from Preston, on 3 August 1968.

The transition from station to car park at Exchange started in 1967, when platforms 1-3 were levelled and tarmacked over. The next decade brought continued decline, as long-distance services were progressively withdrawn. In 1977 what was left of Exchange closed completely to make way for the new underground link line to Central Low Level. The car park that now occupies almost the whole site is pictured in February 2002.

The memory of the L&Y lives on in the grand station and hotel frontage, now incorporated into a modern office development (*left*).
B. Taylor/PDS (2)

GREAT HOWARD STREET was the original passenger terminus of the line from Walton Junction, opened in 1848. Its passenger role lasted only two years but it remained open for goods traffic for well over a century, finally closing in 1963. This view, dated 5 February 1960, shows L&Y 'Pug' No 51227 shunting two 'Shocvans' at Great Howard Street. Both vans are labelled 'Ribble Cement', recalling the days when most rail-borne cement was moved in bagged form, rather than in pressure-discharge tank wagons as it is today.

No trace remains of Great Howard Street today and the photographer had to rely on the close study of Ordnance Survey maps to find the correct location. *J. K. Williams/PDS*

SANDHILLS was the first station on L&Y metals out of Liverpool Exchange, and marked the divergence the Southport line from the main routes to Wigan and Preston. Entering Sandhills with a Liverpool-bound train in this 1960s view is Stanier Class 4 2-6-4T No 42620, at that time allocated to Accrington shed. On the left is a 1939-vintage electric unit heading for Southport.

Sandhills station was completely rebuilt in later BR days, with its original four platforms reduced to a single island platform. The original plans for recasting services after the closure of Exchange envisaged diesel trains to and from Wigan terminating at Sandhills, using a turnback siding just south of the station. However, in the event electrification was extended to Kirkby and the turnback siding was left with no regular use. On 15 February 2002 unit 507011 approaches Sandhills with the 1206 from Ormskirk to Liverpool Central. *Jim Peden/PDS*

BANK HALL: As early as 1850 the L&Y opened its main Liverpool passenger locomotive depot at Bank Hall, in the fork of the lines to Southport and Preston. The original facilities were gradually extended and modernised, culminating in the installation of mechanical coal and ash plants in the 1930s. Bank Hall retained its importance after Nationalisation, with a stud of around 40 locomotives still based there in the late 1950s. The majority were passenger and mixed traffic types, such as 'Jubilee' and Class 5 4-6-0s, but there was also a small allocation of tank engines for shunting in the docks. The photograph shows Johnson 3F 'Jinty' No 47230 passing the entrance to Bank Hall depot on 3 August 1957. Just visible under the coaling stage are two ex-L&Y 'Pugs'.

The inevitable decline in Bank Hall's fortunes took hold in the early 1960s, with the allocation falling to just 18 engines by 1964. Total closure followed on 17 October 1966. The site was subsequently redeveloped as Kirkdale electric multiple unit depot, pictured on 2 March 2002 with unit 508125 passing by with a Kirkby to Liverpool train. A notable resident in the middle distance is stored Class 73 electro-diesel No 73002, one of four members of this class acquired by Merseyrail for departmental duties but latterly retained only for spares and offered for sale in June 2002. *Jim Peden/PDS*

BOOTLE (1): A short stretch of the Liverpool to Southport line through Bootle once boasted six tracks: two for the main line to Southport, two for the branch line from Sandhills to Aintree via Ford, and two for the ex-LNWR line from Edge Hill to Alexandra Dock. Taking the normally goods-only line to Aintree on 23 June 1968 is BR Standard Class 5 No 73069, heading the 'Two Cities' railtour sponsored by the Locomotive Club of Great Britain. This line had lost its regular passenger service as long ago as 1951, although it remained in use after that for Aintree race specials.

Resignalling provided an opportunity to simplify the track layout at Bootle, with the now little-used Aintree line reduced to a single track. The last regular freight services on the line were trip workings to Metal Box at Aintree and Freightliner trains to Aintree Containerbase, both of which ended in the 1980s. The Southport line meanwhile remains as busy as ever. Units 508124 and 508139 head north with the 1237 Liverpool Central to Hall Road train on 2 March 2002. *Dr L. A. Nixon/PDS*

BOOTLE (2): This Edwardian postcard depicts the dawn of the electric age at Bootle Oriel Road, with a Liverpool-bound train about to pick up custom. The station itself was opened in 1876 to replace the less conveniently situated facility at Millers Bridge. Two of the platform signs instruct waiting passengers where to stand in order to board the correct part of the train – a useful aid to timekeeping.

Little remains today of the original buildings at Oriel Road, and the luxury of platform canopies can no longer be justified. Unit 507003 heads a six-car formation working the 1236 Hall Road to Liverpool Central service on 15 February 2002. *John Ryan collection/PDS*

BLUNDELLSANDS & CROSBY: In 1900 the L&Y took the pioneering decision to electrify its busy local lines from Liverpool Exchange to Southport and Aintree. The company chose a 650V DC system, similar to that adopted by the nearby Mersey Railway for its tunnel between Liverpool and Birkenhead. Electric operation out of Exchange was inaugurated in March 1904, using Westinghouse rolling-stock of an unmistakably American design as illustrated in this contemporary postcard. The electrification was so successful that the L&Y increased the number of daily trains on the Southport line from 76 to 131.

The station at Blundellsands & Crosby has changed remarkably little in the last 100 years. The only major difference is the removal of the platform canopies. The line has, however, witnessed several generations of electric rolling-stock. The original American-style stock was augmented by LMS five-coach compartment sets in 1926/27, then replaced by sliding-door units (later Class 502) in 1939. These in turn were replaced by a fleet of Class 507 units from 1978 onwards, later augmented by similar Class 508 units redeployed from the Southern Region. Forming a lunchtime Liverpool to Hall Road service on 15 February 2002 is a six-car formation comprising units 507027 and 508136. *John Ryan collection/PDS*

AINTREE SHED was the L&Y's second locomotive depot on Merseyside and was essentially the freight counterpart of Bank Hall, responsible for traffic to and from the docks and other freight locations such as Fazakerley yard. It was located in the fork of the Ford to Aintree and Ford to Fazakerley lines and comprised an eight-lane shed built in 1886. The LMS added mechanised coaling and ash plants in 1936/37, together with an electrically operated turntable. After Nationalisation the locomotive allocation at Aintree fell only marginally from 55 engines in 1950 to 44 in 1965, but after that the decline was swift and complete closure came on 4 June 1967. The photograph was taken on that final day and shows just three engines – Nos 44809, 44816 and 45147 – standing amid the once bustling tracks. The first two were to be transferred in the following week to Warrington Dallam, while No 45147 had already been withdrawn from service.

Remarkably, the shell of Aintree shed survived for some 29 years after closure, but after its demolition in 1996 the site quickly returned to nature, and today there is no sign of a railway ever having existed here. The adjacent line to Fazakerley was taken out of use in 1987 and officially closed in 1992, while the spur to Aintree (out of sight behind the trees on the left) still appears in the Railtrack Route Directory of January 2002 despite having been disused for many years. *Jim Peden/PDS*

MAGHULL: The L&Y opened its line to Aintree and Ormskirk in 1849. For just over half a century all trains were steam-worked, but following the success of electrification on the Southport line the conductor rails were extended to Aintree in 1906, to Maghull in 1909 and to Ormskirk in 1913. This scene at Maghull was captured shortly before the electrics arrived.

Today, Maghull station retains its original footbridge and station building, the latter somewhat altered but still with two of its original chimney pots. The line lost its through Liverpool to Preston workings in 1970, but electric trains continue to provide a frequent service between Liverpool and Ormskirk. A visit to Maghull on 2 March 2002 found unit No 507031 bringing up the rear of a six-car formation working the 0825 Liverpool Central to Ormskirk service, and sister unit No 507011 forming the 0836 from Ormskirk to Liverpool Central. *John Ryan collection/PDS*

PRESTON ROAD/RICE LANE: The line from Walton Junction to Kirkby was opened in 1848 as part of the L&Y main line from Liverpool Great Howard Street (later Exchange) to Lostock Junction near Bolton. Preston Road was the first station beyond Walton Junction, and is pictured here in the 1920s.

Goods facilities were withdrawn from Preston Road in 1964 and the Liverpool-bound platform was subsequently extended to enable closure of the portion under the (widened) road bridge. The line through Preston Road was electrified in 1977 and the station was named Rice Lane in 1984. Unit No 507021 forms the 1648 Kirkby to Liverpool Central service on 6 May 2002. *Stations UK/PDS*

KIRKBY
Pears Soap
CROSSLEY'S
GAS AND OIL ENGINES
PATENT GAS PLANTS
WATCHES
PEARS
KIRKBY STATION

KIRKBY: The station staff stand characteristically to attention in this turn-of-the-last-century view of Kirkby. In those days Kirkby itself was a small rural settlement and the station was a relatively minor intermediate location on the L&Y main line from Liverpool to Bolton and Manchester.

The decline of the main line through Kirkby began in 1968 when BR announced that the Pemberton loop was to go, forcing Manchester trains to run via Wigan Wallgate and lengthening their journey by several minutes. A decade later, as part of the Merseyside electrification scheme, Kirkby benefited from a new station on the other side of the road bridge. However, at the same time through running to Wigan became impossible as buffer stops were placed on the former 'up' line, effectively making the station into two adjoining termini, diesel units being provided for a separate service between Kirkby and Wigan. The first of the present-day photographs, dated 2 March 2002, shows the former station access ramp, now abandoned but with cobbles still in place. The platform here is still used by the diesel service to Wigan. The third photograph, dated 6 May 2002, shows the new station building and platform viewed from the road bridge, with unit 507017 having just arrived with the 1220 service from Liverpool Central. *Stations UK/PDS*

Cheshire Lines

HUSKISSON: Keen to tap the lucrative market for freight to and from the docks, as well as traffic to and from the city itself, the Cheshire Lines Committee (CLC) opened its North Liverpool terminus at Huskisson in 1880. It was served by a south-facing spur from the North Liverpool Extension line (Hunts Cross to Aintree) and its approach tracks ran parallel to, but at a lower level than, the L&Y line into Liverpool Exchange. Passenger services to Huskisson lasted only five years, but goods traffic thrived for the best part of a century. Ex-L&Y Class 0F 0-4-0 'Pug' No 51227 arrives at Huskisson with wagons from Sandon Dock in October 1959.

Huskisson finally closed in 1975. Although the approach trackbed is still recognisable in places, the goods depot site has been completely redeveloped, as this March 2002 view shows. *John Ryan collection/PDS*

WALTON-ON-THE-HILL was the smaller of the two CLC sheds in Liverpool, opened in May 1881. The shed's decline began shortly after Nationalisation: its six-track dead-end building was reduced to take just four tracks in 1952, and its turntable was taken out of commission later in the same decade. By the date of the photograph, 21 June 1957, the original ex-CLC locomotive allocation had been largely supplanted by ex-LMS types. Those visible here include Fowler Class 4F 0-6-0 Nos 44291, 44541, 43843 and 44481.

Walton-on-the-Hill shed closed completely in December 1963. Both the shed site and the adjacent Huskisson branch trackbed have been swallowed up by a modern housing development, pictured here in March 2002. *Jim Peden/PDS*

AINTREE CENTRAL: The CLC opened its extension to Aintree Central in 1880 and onwards to Southport Lord Street in 1884, giving the company access to substantial but largely seasonal seaside traffic. The Southport extension was not a great success and the line was cut back to Aintree Central in 1952. Fairburn 2-6-4T No 42113 stands at Aintree Central with the 12.07pm service from Manchester Central on 5 November 1960. Just visible on the skyline is the coaling plant of Aintree shed.

The official closure date for Aintree Central was 7 November 1960, just two days after the date of the 'past' photograph. However, the four-platform terminus remained in use for race specials until 1963. Today the trackbed provides road access to an industrial estate, as pictured on 2 March 2002. *T. J. Edgington/PDS*

KNOTTY ASH & STANLEY was one of six intermediate stations between Hunts Cross and Aintree on the CLC North Liverpool Extension line. The passenger platforms are pictured on 20 April 1954, by which time the ex-CLC route beyond Aintree had closed and traffic on the remaining section was ominously sparse.

Regular passenger services between Gateacre and Aintree finished on 7 November 1960, bringing the closure of Knotty Ash and all other intermediate stations. However, the nearby coal yard remained in use for several more years. Today the Liverpool Loop Line cycleway uses the former southbound platform, as pictured in March 2002. *H. C. Casserley/PDS*

GATEACRE FOR WOOLTON (1): The Grand National at Aintree brought renewed life to the former CLC North Liverpool Extension line, with specials operating to Aintree Central from various locations. 'Black Five' 4-6-0 No 44966, allocated to Saltley, speeds through Gateacre with a racegoers' train from Birmingham New Street on 29 March 1958. Specials such as this continued to operate until 1963, three years after the end of regular passenger workings north of Gateacre.

Gateacre survived as a terminus for local trains from Liverpool Central (High Level) until 1972. Through freight services finished a few years later and the way was then clear to convert the line into a popular footpath and cycleway, known as the Liverpool Loop Line. The present-day view is dated 2 March 2002. *Jim Peden/PDS*

GATEACRE FOR WOOLTON (2): For a relatively minor station, Gateacre & Woolton boasted an imposing entrance, as shown in this turn-of-the-last-century postcard. Commercial premises now occupy the site, pictured in December 2001. Access to the footpath and cycleway on the former trackbed is by means of an incline on the other side of the road, behind the photographer. *John Ryan collection/PDS*

HALEWOOD NORTH JUNCTION: Stanier 8F 2-8-0 No 48457 heads north at Halewood North Junction with a typical mixed freight working, likely to have been bound for Huskisson, on 24 April 1962. At that time No 48457 was allocated to Edge Hill, the largest and most important of the Liverpool area sheds.

In March 2002 the site of Halewood North Junction could be located only by careful use of an Ordnance Survey map. The Liverpool Loop Line cycleway threads its way through a thicket of bramble, birch and willow that has quickly colonised the abandoned trackbed. Hopes of a railway revival here, as proposed in the ambitious Outer Rail Loop scheme of the mid-1970s, seem as remote as ever. *J. F. Ward/PDS*

HUNTS CROSS EAST JUNCTION: The beginnings of track rationalisation are already evident in this 1968 view of Hunts Cross East Junction, where the North Liverpool Extension to Huskisson and Aintree diverged from the CLC Liverpool-Manchester line. The four-track formation is a reminder of more prosperous times, when the CLC needed to ensure swift passage for its hourly-interval expresses between Liverpool and Manchester – reputedly the fastest regular daily expresses in the world – alongside frequent goods and local passenger workings.

By the mid-1970s the CLC line carried only DMU-operated passenger services between Liverpool and Manchester, with expresses concentrated on the former LNWR route and almost all freight diverted or withdrawn. Today the line once again carries long-distance trains, but all are operated by units. One of the first batch of 'Sprinters', Class 150 No 150140, heads towards Liverpool on 2 March 2002 with an afternoon stopping train from Manchester. *Stations UK/PDS*

GARSTON station opened in 1874 when the CLC inaugurated its through passenger services between Liverpool Central and Manchester Central. In those days there was no competition from cars or lorries, but railway rivalry was intense, with the L&Y and LNWR already operating between the North West's two premier cities. After Nationalisation, through services between Liverpool and Manchester continued to operate on all three routes, although eventually most long-distance expresses were concentrated on the LNWR route. On 21 April 1950 Class 2P 4-4-0 No 40655 enters Garston station with the 3.30pm Liverpool to Manchester train.

Garston station closed in 1972 when the service to Gateacre ended. It then re-opened in March 1978 as the terminus of the newly extended Northern Line electric service from Southport via central Liverpool. This was extended in 1983 from Garston to Hunts Cross, connecting with diesel trains from Liverpool Lime Street to Warrington and Manchester. Plans for a further extension of the third rail to Hough Green were thwarted by cash shortages. On 15 December 2001 Class 507 unit No 507029 calls at Garston forming the 1201 service from Southport to Hunts Cross. Garston signal box has long since disappeared, and the whole line from Liverpool Central is now controlled from Hunts Cross. In 2002 there was a proposal to relocate Garston station 200 yards towards Hunts Cross, forming an interchange with Allerton. *H. C. Casserley/PDS*

MERSEY ROAD was one of six intermediate stations between Liverpool Central and Garston. This postcard scene is likely to have been taken around the turn of the last century, although it does not show the name change to Mersey Road & Aigburth that took place in 1880.

A further change of name to Aigburth came in 1978 when the Garston line was re-opened and electrified. Despite the six-year period of closure, the station building remained intact, and at least some of the canopy ironwork appears to be original too. Unit 508114 calls with a Southport to Hunts Cross service on 15 December 2001. *John Ryan collection/PDS*

BRUNSWICK: Although the first terminus of the Garston & Liverpool Railway – later to become part of the CLC – was at Brunswick, opened in 1864, it was made redundant just ten years later by the extension from Brunswick to Liverpool Central. However, for the best part of a century Brunswick remained an important location for goods traffic, providing access to the southern end of the docks system as well as to local terminals. The last source of traffic was an oil storage terminal, which closed in the late 1970s; the working timetable for 1972 still shows a daily departure from Brunswick to Courtaulds at Holywell Junction. This view, dated 5 September 1976, shows the connection to Brunswick goods depot intact but little used, while the main line to Liverpool Central had been disused since the Gateacre service finished in 1972.

The present-day photograph of Brunswick shows a rare and refreshing example of regeneration. Although there is no freight traffic, Merseyrail has opened a new passenger station to serve local industry and housing, breaking the 3-mile gap between St Michaels and Liverpool Central. Class 507 unit No 507024 forms a lunchtime train from Hunts Cross to Southport on 20 December 2001. *J. A. Sommerfield/PDS*

BRUNSWICK SHED: This evocative scene at Brunswick depicts the former CLC shed in its LNER years, just before the outbreak of the Second World War. The shed occupied a narrow site hewn out of the sandstone, with the entrance to Dingle Tunnel immediately behind the photographer. Foot access was down the flight of 92 steps visible on the right. The shed provided traction both for the Liverpool-Manchester passenger service and for substantial goods traffic to and from the nearby docks. As with the other CLC shed in Liverpool, Walton-on-the-Hill, the locomotive allocation at Brunswick changed gradually from ex-LNER to ex-LMS types.

The retaining wall provides a visual link with the present-day picture, dated 20 December 2001. The tracks of the Liverpool-Garston line are still there, but well hidden behind the barrage of high-security fencing and undergrowth. The public footbridge, meanwhile, has been demolished, evidently without the provision of an alternative route. *Stations UK/PDS*

LIVERPOOL
CENTRAL
42949
8E

LIVERPOOL CENTRAL (1): Opened in 1874, Central (High Level) was the third and last of Liverpool's principal main-line termini. It was built on a cramped site, with platforms of varying lengths to make the most of the available space, and its approaches were entirely in tunnel. After Nationalisation, Central's fortunes declined in tune with the gradual run-down of the former CLC and Great Central systems, and services were eventually cut back to the core route to Manchester via Warrington and the short branch to Gateacre. The photograph shows Stanier 5MT 'Mogul' 2-6-0 No 42949 waiting to leave Central with the 11.43am train to Stockport on 22 August 1955.

After closure in 1972 the concourse area of Liverpool Central was redeveloped as a shopping precinct, while most of the remainder of the site became a car park. Trains on the former CLC line now run underground at this point, serving Central Low Level station, which was rebuilt as part of the 1970s Loop and Link Line project. *Brian Morrison/PDS*

LIVERPOOL CENTRAL (2): In its twilight years, Central High Level was served mainly by diesel multiple units. What appears to be a Derby-built unit (later Class 108) stands alongside platform 2 on 29 April 1966, waiting to return to Manchester. The station staff seem to be making a thorough job of checking tickets.

The same location is pictured on 15 February 2002. The only visual link between the old and new pictures is the steel bridge carrying Newington Street across the station hollow. *Ian Holt/PDS*

The London & North Western Railway

LIVERPOOL LIME STREET: The LNWR built its first terminus at Lime Street in 1836, but the present structure dates back to 1851. The long train shed with its impressive arched façade was one of the first in Britain to have an iron framework and was listed by the LNWR as one of its principal engineering works. But regular steam haulage did not come to Lime Street until 1870: before that time trains on the incline from Edge Hill were rope-worked. The frontage is pictured on 11 September 1955, with the original vehicular entrance still visible just to the left of the tram.

Lime Street was the only main-line terminus in Liverpool to last the whole of the 20th century. The station concourse and frontage were given a multi-million pound facelift in the 1980s, while beneath the ground the construction of the Loop Line in the 1970s gave Lime Street its first rail link with the Wirral. The modern scene is dated 15 February 2002. *B. Mettam/PDS*

CROWN STREET: One of the oldest railway locations in Britain was Crown Street, opened in 1830 as the original terminus of the world-famous Liverpool & Manchester Railway. Its passenger role lasted only six years, as the LNWR was soon to extend its tracks through the deep sandstone cutting to Lime Street. However, Crown Street remained open as a goods station for another 142 years, served by a short spur from the main line at Edge Hill. This 1962 view shows one of the diminutive 0-4-0 diesel shunters that had only recently taken over from steam traction. The chimney is an air vent for the railway tunnel to Wapping, formerly used by docks freight traffic.

Crown Street closed to goods in 1972 and the site was subsequently turned into a pleasant public open space, pictured here in December 2001. The only hint of a former railway link is the air vent, surviving intact, as does the railway tunnel itself. *C. H. A. Townley/PDS*

EDGE HILL (1): Edge Hill station was once a three-way junction with lines to Lime Street, Wapping and Riverside, although platforms were only located on the Lime Street tracks. A pair of ex-LNWR 7F 0-8-0 locomotives, Nos 49314 and 49082, are pictured coupling on to a Northern Rubber Company excursion train bound for Riverside on 4 September 1954. The 2½-mile branch from Edge Hill to Riverside had a ruling gradient of 1 in 60 and was almost entirely in tunnel, just like the adjacent branch to Wapping. Edge Hill at this time was a major gathering point for goods traffic to and from the docks, most of it conveyed in individual wagonloads such as the rake seen on the left.

The Riverside branch closed in 1971, but the sidings on the north side of Edge Hill station are still used today by locomotives running round freight trains to and from the Bootle branch. Loadhaul-liveried No 56109 is seen running round a train of empty MEA box wagons bound for Liverpool Bulk Terminal on 20 December 2001. *E. Stephens/PDS*

EDGE HILL (2): Our second view at Edge Hill was taken from the same vantage point but facing in the opposite direction. A pair of main-line locomotives, with ex-LNER 'D1' 4-4-0 No 62663 *Prince Albert* nearest the camera, have just uncoupled from the Riverside-bound Northern Rubber Company excursion train on 4 September 1954. The mouth of Waterloo Tunnel of the Riverside branch is just to the right of the signal box but obscured by steam.

Only a short length of track remains in Waterloo Tunnel today, used as a headshunt for trains running round in Tuebrook sidings. The 'present' photograph is dated 20 December 2001. *E. Stephens/PDS*

EDGE HILL (3): A rare survivor of a long-obsolete locomotive class was ex-Lancashire & Yorkshire Railway 0-4-4T No 925, retained at Edge Hill for carriage heating purposes. It is pictured in 1964 in the company of two six-wheeled brake-vans.

The demolition of Edge Hill carriage shed opened up a new view of the Victorian station buildings at Edge Hill station. A Class 142 'Pacer' unit is just departing from platform 3 with an eastbound local service on 20 December 2001. *Jim Peden collection/PDS*

EDGE HILL (4): 'Jubilee' 4-6-0 No 45581 *Bihar and Orissa* heads east from Edge Hill with a Liverpool to Newcastle express on 22 August 1955. At this time Edge Hill boasted an intricate arrangement of sidings, loops and flyovers, not to mention one of the principal engine sheds on the London Midland Region with an allocation of over 100 locomotives.

Access to the same location in 2002 was not possible, but this view dated 2 April 1986 still makes an interesting comparison. The 1450 Liverpool Lime Street to Wigan North Western stopper is formed by one of the then commonplace Class 108 DMUs, while the resident pilot locomotive for Edge Hill coal concentration depot – since closed – is visible on the left. The disused gantries are a reminder that a short stretch of the Manchester line – as far as Bootle Branch Junction – was included in the 1960s Crewe to Liverpool electrification scheme. Much of the land beside the railway at this point has now been taken up by the Wavertree Technology Park, which even gained its own passenger station in August 2000. *Brian Morrison/PDS*

PIGHUE LANE JUNCTION: The layout of railway lines around Edge Hill was arguably the most intricate on Merseyside, with curves and flyovers providing direct connections between the various routes. Pighue Lane Junction was the point where the Waterloo independent lines diverged from the east-to-north curve connecting Olive Mount Junction with Edge Lane Junction. A 'Jinty' 0-6-0T is pictured hauling a mixed rake of coal wagons on to the Waterloo independent lines in about 1960.

The Waterloo independent lines were taken out of use in 1976, while the curve between Olive Mount Junction and Edge Lane Junction lasted until 1987. After that time all trains to and from the docks had to reverse in the Edge Hill area – either at Tuebrook sidings on the north side of the line or at Gullet sidings on the south side. The closure of the curve was surprising in view of the growth in freight volume to and from Liverpool Bulk Terminal and Seaforth since the 1980s. Recently Railtrack has indicated a desire to re-open the curve, but at the time of writing it is unclear where the money would come from. *Jim Peden/PDS*

HUYTON QUARRY once marked the end of the quadruple track section from Lime Street, completed by the LNWR in 1871 to cope with increasing volumes of traffic. The station at Huyton Quarry was an early casualty of BR cutbacks, closing to passengers and goods in 1958. However, the location retained its signal box into the 1960s, as it was the junction for the Willis branch to Cronton colliery. This 1966 picture shows the Willis branch diverging to the left in the middle distance.

Today it is hard to believe that anything more than plain double track ever existed at Huyton Quarry, and trees such as birch and willow have quickly colonised the trackside. 'Pacer' unit 142043 recedes towards Liverpool with an early morning stopping train from Manchester Victoria on 2 March 2002. *Jim Peden collection/PDS*

ALLERTON STATION: The link from Edge Hill to Allerton and Speke, now part of the Liverpool to Crewe main line, was a comparatively late addition to the Merseyside railway network, opening to traffic in 1864. The track was quadrupled in 1891 to cope with rising traffic levels. BR Standard 4-6-0 No 75013 passes Allerton with an excursion train on 27 August 1954.

The line from Edge Hill to Allerton gained additional traffic when trains to and from the ex-CLC Warrington line were diverted to Lime Street instead of Central. Central Trains 'Super Sprinter' No 156409 passes through with the 1052 Liverpool to Norwich service on 20 December 2001 – a journey of nearly 6 hours by diesel multiple unit! *Jim Peden/PDS*

ALLERTON JUNCTION: 'Royal Scot' 4-6-0 No 46110 *Grenadier Guardsman* passes Allerton Junction with the up 'Manxman' on 3 July 1954. The 'Royal Scot' Class was a familiar traction type on the West Coast Main Line in the 1950s, and around a dozen examples were allocated to Edge Hill. The tracks curving round to the left form the spur to Garston Junction, giving access to Garston Docks.

Electrification has since transformed the scene at Allerton Junction, but the track layout remains basically unchanged – even though the spur to Garston Junction sees little use these days. Access to the 'past' vantage point is no longer possible – indeed, one of the striking differences between the two pictures is the removal of the public footbridge – so the 'present' view is taken from the opposite side of the line. An afternoon Liverpool to London train passes the junction on 20 December 2001. *Jim Peden/PDS*

GARSTON DOCK: The first railway route to Liverpool from the Runcorn direction was the line opened by the St Helens & Runcorn Gap Railway in 1852 from Runcorn to Garston Dock. The section between Speke Junction and Garston Dock was downgraded to branch status 12 years later when the LNWR opened its main line from Speke Junction to Edge Hill, the LNWR having by this time absorbed the St Helens & Runcorn Gap Railway. There was also a spur enabling through running from Garston Dock to Allerton. Garston Dock later became an end-on junction with the CLC when the CLC opened a spur from Cressington Junction on its Liverpool to Garston main line. However, despite its apparently pivotal location, Garston Dock had little importance as a passenger location. The CLC withdrew its link from Cressington after just a few years and scheduled passenger services from Allerton to Garston Dock ceased in 1947. The photograph shows the disused platforms in 1949.

After losing its passenger services, the line from Speke Junction to Cressington Junction continued to provide a connection for freight between the former LNWR and CLC lines until the section between Garston Dock Road and Cressington Junction closed completely in 1977. Part of the formation was then used for the re-routed A561 trunk road, as pictured in December 2001. *Stations UK/PDS*

GARSTON CHURCH ROAD was the only intermediate station on the LNWR Garston Dock branch. It had an even shorter life than Garston Dock itself, opening in 1881 and closing in 1939. This turn-of-the-last-century postcard view shows Church Road station with the station staff adopting the characteristic pose of early photography. By this time most railway passengers to and from Garston would have used the nearby CLC station on the Liverpool to Halewood line. Garston Dock meanwhile grew in importance as a freight location, predominantly for coal but also handling traffic as diverse as bananas, china clay and timber.

In the 1960s Garston Freightliner terminal was built adjacent to the site of Garston Church Road station. Until the 1970s some trains between Garston and Trafford Park ran via the now closed link to Cressington and the CLC route, but today all trains arrive and depart via Speke Junction, with the Allerton curve retained for occasional non-timetabled movements. The coal terminal at Garston Dock benefited from major investment in hopper discharge facilities in 1981 but this traffic ceased altogether a decade later, leaving Freightliner as the only rail freight operator in the area. The east end of the Freightliner terminal is pictured on 20 December 2001, with pilot loco No 08891 partly concealed by an intermodal wagon. *John Ryan collection/PDS*

The blood of the martyrs
is the seed of Christians
Tertullian (circa 160-220)

Please pray for these 25 servants of the Church who lost their lives for the Lord in mission territories in 2002:

Isaias Duarte Cancino, archbishop, Colombia, March 16
Declan O'Toole, priest, Uganda, March 21
Boniface, priest, Congo, March 24
Juan Ramon Nunez, priest, Argentina, April 6
Roger Morin, priest, Madagascar, April 12
Alois Lintner, priest, Brazil, May 16
Arley Arias Garcia, priest, Colombia, May 18
Jorge Altafulla, priest, Panama, May 19
Jose Ilario Arango, priest, Colombia, June 27
Marta Ines Velez Serna, sister, Colombia, July 14
Carlos Herrao Jimenez, seminarian, Colombia, July 21
Ivo M Dominique Lascanne, brother, Cameroon, July 30
Pierre Tondo, priest, Burundi, August 5
Jean Guth, priest, Congo, August 10
Cecilia, sister, Baghdad, August 15
Augustin Geve, priest, Solomon Islands, August 20
Leonardo Muakalia Livongue, seminarian, Angola, September 8
Jose Luis Arroyave, priest, Colombia, September 20
Jorge Sanchez Ramirez, priest, Colombia, September 27
Jose Luis Cardenas, priest, Colombia, October 17
Gabriel Arias Posadas, priest, Colombia, October 18
Alberto Neri Fernandez, layman, Brazil, October 19
Declan Collins, priest, South Africa, November 16
James Iyere, priest, Central African Republic, November 29
Jean-Claude Kilamong, priest, Central African Republic, December 8

Remember all those who are similarly tested for their faith.

Mission

Association for the Propagation of the Faith (APF)
Mill Hill Missionaries (MHM)
Registered Charities, with your generous help supporting all Catholic missions

SPEKE: 'Black Five' 4-6-0 No 45417 and BR Standard 2-10-0 No 92117 pass Speke with 4F27, the 9.20am Brunswick to Shotwick block oil train, on 1 March 1967. This working conveyed 18 45-ton tank wagons with fuel oil for the John Summers steelworks. It was a regular candidate for double heading until steam was finally ousted by diesel traction.

Oil traffic from Brunswick storage terminal ceased in the 1970s, but the main line continues to handle a range of freight flows, including containers to and from Garston and Seaforth and automotive traffic to and from Garston. Recently delivered Freightliner loco No 66551 passes Speke with an additional working from Seaforth to Crewe on the morning of 20 December 2001. *John Feild/PDS*

Liverpool Docks and the Overhead Railway

LIVERPOOL DOCKS: This classic view from the roof of the Royal Liver Building, dated June 1956, provides a glimpse of Liverpool's thriving docklands before the decline of the 1960s and 1970s. Running prominently from centre to bottom right is the Liverpool Overhead Railway, just six months before its untimely closure. At street level in the foreground a fragment of the extensive Mersey Docks & Harbour Board (MDHB) system is visible. In 1956 most of the docks still had rail access, and there were railway-owned public goods depots at Alexandra Dock, Bankfield, Great Howard Street, Langton Dock, North Docks, North Mersey, Pier Head, Sandon Dock, Wapping and Waterloo Dock.

In the last 46 years all traces of the railway have disappeared and most of the buildings have changed too. The growth of road transport is amply demonstrated by the widening of New Quay to eight lanes and by the extensive car parks, partly occupying the site of Princes Dock. Maritime activity is now concentrated some distance further north. *Jim Peden/PDS*

WAPPING: The MDHB system formed a through route from Alexandra Dock in the north to Brunswick in the south, a distance of about 5½ miles. It gave access to numerous docks, private sidings and railway goods depots along the way, as well as enjoying direct links with the LNWR, L&Y and CLC systems. Ex-L&Y Class 0F 0-4-0 'Pug' No 51232 pauses during shunting duties at Wapping on 29 October 1960. The tracks in the foreground led to the ex-LNWR goods depot named Park Lane, which also had direct main-line access from Edge Hill. By the date of this photograph only three 'Pugs' were based at Bank Hall shed for work in the docks, and all were gone by the end of 1962.

The stone tower on the right is the only point of reference shared by the old photograph and the present-day one dated February 2002. The road behind the tower gives access to the revitalised Albert Dock complex. *Jim Peden/PDS*

PIER HEAD (1): It seems hard to imagine today that railway lines once ran alongside Strand Street and New Quay, allowing goods trains – albeit slow-moving ones – to mingle with pedestrians and bicycles. Until dieselisation came in the early 1960s all trains were worked by ex-L&Y 'Pugs', allocated to Bank Hall shed because of its proximity to Liverpool's docklands. A total of 11 'Pugs' were based there in 1950, reduced to eight in 1959. They were among the smallest engines owned by British Railways, and by the time of their withdrawal they were also among the oldest, having been introduced in 1891. No 51253 passes the Cunard Building near Pier Head on 23 January 1960.

The same scene is pictured in February 2002, all traces of the railway having long since disappeared. *Jim Peden/PDS*

PIER HEAD (2): The Liverpool Overhead Railway (LOR) opened in 1893 and was the world's first urban elevated electric railway. It was also the first railway in Britain to have automatic daylight colour light signals. The 6½-mile line ran from Seaforth in the north to Dingle in the south, and served 16 intermediate stations. It was designed essentially as a commuter line for people working in the docks – hence its nickname 'the Dockers' Umbrella' – but it also became increasingly popular with tourists, as it offered panoramic views of the docks and ships on the Mersey. The LOR was severely damaged during the Second World War but, although there were behind-the-scenes proposals to close it, the arguments for its repair and retention at that time were compelling and full services were restored as quickly as practicable. A standard three-coach train is pictured on the section above New Quay, just north of Pier Head station, in 1952.

Unfortunately the fortunes of the LOR declined sharply in the 1950s. Engineers discovered severe corrosion in parts of the elevated structure and, despite buoyant traffic levels – it carried 9 million passengers in its last year of operation – the LOR was declared to be beyond economic repair. The last train ran on 30 December 1956 and virtually all traces of the line were soon removed. The modern photograph dated 15 February 2002 shows the complete transformation that has taken place on New Quay. *R. K. Blencowe collection/PDS*

SEAFORTH & LITHERLAND (1): A few years after its opening, the LOR was extended northwards from its original terminus at Seaforth Sands to join up with the L&Y Southport line at Seaforth & Litherland station. One of the original LOR two-car sets of 1892, with a middle trailer added, is about to depart for Dingle on 31 July 1955, the penultimate year of LOR operation. Seaforth & Litherland and Dingle were the only stations served by the LOR that were not elevated; the terminus at Dingle was actually at the end of a half-mile-long tunnel.

The track at Seaforth & Litherland once used by terminating LOR trains is now the 'down' running line for Merseyrail trains to Southport. Unit No 507010 calls with the 1237 service from Liverpool Central to Hall Road on 15 February 2002. *R. K. Blencowe collection/PDS*

SEAFORTH & LITHERLAND (2): BR semaphore signals controlled the arrival and departure of LOR trains at Seaforth & Litherland station. This south-facing view, dated 31 July 1955, shows a service arriving from Dingle past a later version of the signals seen in the previous photograph, having used the curve just visible on the right-hand side. The main line signals are 'off' for a Liverpool-bound express.

The LOR curve has long gone, but the bridge carrying the disused Sandhills to Aintree line is still visible on the skyline. Two Class 507 units call with the 1251 Hall Road to Liverpool Central service on 15 February 2002. *R. K. Blencowe collection/PDS*

RIVERSIDE station was unusual in that it was owned by the MDHB rather than by any of the railway companies, and it never had a scheduled passenger service. Instead it handled special trains connecting with transatlantic sailings. Sandwiched on a narrow site between Princes Dock and the landing stage, Riverside had three platform faces spanned by a substantial roof, as pictured in this photograph of No 47487 with the Liverpool University Public Transport Society 'Liverpool Suburban' railtour on 13 June 1964.

Airline competition led to the loss of liner traffic from Liverpool, and the closure of Riverside station followed in March 1971. The structure remained in situ throughout the 1990s, but was eventually demolished to make way for the Isle of Man Steam Packet terminal, pictured here in February 2002. *Ian Holt/PDS*

PRINCES DOCK: Trains to Riverside descended the 2-mile inclined tunnel from Edge Hill to Waterloo Goods before crossing the MDHB goods lines and running a short distance along the west side of Princes Dock. 'Jubilee' 4-6-0 No 45629 *Straits Settlements*, allocated to Crewe North shed, passes Princes Dock with a Riverside-bound working on 20 July 1959.

Three decades after closure the line of route of the Riverside branch is still visible at the entrance to Princes Dock. The former warehouses beside Waterloo Dock have been retained and converted into flats, as seen in the 'present' photograph dated 15 February 2002. *Jim Peden/PDS*

SANDON DOCK: Direct rail access to the various docks was complemented by public goods depots operated not just by the LNWR, L&Y and CLC but also by companies without their own rail access to Merseyside, including the Great Central and the Midland Railway. 'Pug' No 51229 is on duty at the former Midland Railway depot at Sandon Dock on 27 February 1960. This location had access from the CLC goods station at Huskisson, as well as from the MDHB system.

Sandon Dock goods depot closed in February 1969, towards the end of the long period of decline in Liverpool's dockland railways. An industrial estate now occupies its site, illustrated on 15 February 2002. *J. K. Williams/PDS*

ALEXANDRA DOCK: The LNWR inaugurated passenger services on its Bootle branch from Edge Hill to Canada Dock in 1870, with the spur to Alexandra Dock following in 1881. The route became an important one for goods traffic to and from the north docks, but passenger traffic was insubstantial and Canada Dock and Alexandra Dock stations were closed in 1941 and 1949 respectively. The structure at Alexandra Dock remained intact for a remarkably long time; it is pictured on 13 June 1964 with No 47487 stopping for a photo-call on the 'Liverpool Suburban' railtour.

By the end of the 1960s the Bootle branch provided the only means of access to the MDHB system. Further decline was inevitable and the MDHB system handled its last rail freight consignment in 1973. But revival came just a few years later, thanks to the development of Liverpool Freeport and Seaforth container terminal. The Alexandra Dock branch was revived and regular Freightliner services to Seaforth commenced in February 1980. Flows of coal, steel and scrap metal to and from the docks were subsequently acquired, and to cope with the increased traffic BR restored the double track between Bootle Junction and Alexandra Dock in 1992. The modern view is dated 2 March 2002.

Situated just to the right of the two main views of Alexandra Dock was the Post Office terminal, still handling regular traffic in 1986 but reduced to little more than an empty shed in its later years, as seen in the third photograph. Class 31 No 31434 departs from Alexandra Dock with 'target 73' to Edge Hill Downhill Sidings on the evening of 2 April 1986. *D. Hampson/PDS*

NORTH MERSEY GOODS: Rail-borne goods traffic carried by the MDHB declined from over 4 million tons in 1944 to 150,000 tons in 1972. One of the last dockside locations to handle regular traffic was the former L&Y goods depot at North Mersey, serving Alexandra, Hornby and Gladstone Docks. Class 08 shunter No D3855 is stabled at North Mersey Goods on 19 August 1971, two years before closure of this last remnant of the MDHB network.

The site of North Mersey Goods is now situated within the docks estate. Rails returned with the opening of the coal-handling terminal at Gladstone Dock, pictured here on 2 March 2002. Surprisingly, the south end of the warehouse labelled 'East Hornby Dock' in the old photograph is still visible today, albeit partly obscured by a more recent building. *J. A. Sommerfield/PDS*

LIVERPOOL BULK TERMINAL: The shift towards the use of imported coal in UK power stations led to the building of several new or enhanced coal import terminals in the late 1980s and 1990s. Powergen decided to use Gladstone Dock as its principal import terminal for Fiddlers Ferry power station and opened a new rail loading facility there in 1988. Initially the coal was loaded by mechanical shovel from the trackside, as pictured on 19 May 1990.

Once it became clear that imported coal was here to stay, Powergen invested £40 million in upgrading its Gladstone Dock facility, with new conveyors and automated loading apparatus capable of handling 5 million tonnes of coal a year. Now known as Liverpool Bulk Terminal, the new facility received its first test train on 21 July 1993. The backbone of the operation is still imported coal for Fiddlers Ferry, but in 2000-02 there were also flows to other power stations such as Rugeley and industrial coal to cement works at Penyffordd and Clitheroe. The photograph, dated 1 June 1999, shows Class 66 No 66014 with a rake of MEAs, which will form the 1430 departure to Clitheroe. *Both PDS*

Hooton to Rock Ferry

HOOTON (1): The station dates back to the first railway on the Wirral, when the line from Chester to Birkenhead was opened in 1840. It became a junction in 1863, with the line to Helsby, followed three years later by the branch to Parkgate on Deeside (which was extended to West Kirby 20 years later). At one time there were six through platforms together with a bay used for the trains to Ellesmere Port and Helsby. The two platforms on the left were used primarily for the West Kirby branch, which had closed to passengers in 1956 but remained open when our 'past' picture was taken on 2 June 1961, prior to complete closure the following year. An ex-LMS 2-6-4T can be seen at the far end on the left, and a train with parcels vans attached stands in the adjacent platform.

Today the station consists of just one island platform, the other having been reduced to half width; only two platforms are in regular use, as seen in the photograph taken on 27 February 2002, showing Class 508 No 508134 with a service to Ellesmere Port. The station building and entrance are little changed. *H. C. Casserley/JCH*

HOOTON (2): Looking south on 2 June 1961, BR Standard 2-6-2T No 84003 enters the station with the 5.10pm Stanlow to Birkenhead train, while on the left an ex-LMS Stanier 2-6-0 of taper boiler design, No 42969, is about to depart. Note the water columns on each platform.

Since the days when the station was a busy double junction, the tracks have been rationalised down to just two through lines, together with one line that is buffered at the north end of the station from the Chester direction and can be used as a bay, and a parallel line that terminates beyond the station on the Rock Ferry side, both having been through lines at one time but neither seeing much use today. In the 'present' picture, taken on 2 July 2002, Class 508 No 508128 approaches with a Liverpool service. The two up signals have junction 'feathers' for the Ellesmere Port/Helsby line. *H. C. Casserley/JCH*

BROMBOROUGH: In 1907/8 the Chester to Birkenhead line was quadrupled between Ledsham, just south of Hooton, and Green Lane (Birkenhead), enabling some degree of segregation for express passenger, local passenger and freight services. Stanier 2-6-4T No 42569 calls at the down fast platform at Bromborough with the 6.35pm Chester General to Birkenhead Woodside train on 2 June 1961.

With the loss of main-line passenger services and the gradual run-down of freight, the line reverted to double track in the 1960s, and today there is ample capacity for the line's basic 15-minute service; anything other than a Class 507 or 508 electric unit on this stretch is very rare indeed. Unit 507101 calls with the 1550 Chester to Liverpool service on 25 October 2001. *H. C. Casserley/PDS*

BEBINGTON station dates right back to the beginnings of the Chester & Birkenhead Railway in 1840, becoming GW&LNWR Joint in 1860. It was known as Bebington & New Ferry from 1895 until 1974. The line was doubled in 1847, and with the considerable increase in traffic was quadrupled in the 1902-10 period. This entailed enlargement of the stations, and Bebington gained an island platform. Subsequently, after the Second World War,

when freight diminished, it reverted to double track, and the platform buildings were demolished and replaced by the bus-shelter type. In our 'past' picture we see an ex-LMS 0-6-0T 'Jinty' heading north, perhaps returning to Mollington Street shed.

As can be seen in the 'present' picture, taken on 2 July 2002, there is little to link the two views other than the ¼ milepost at the end of the platform. *Dr L. A. Nixon/JCH*

ROCK FERRY (1): When opened in 1862, Rock Ferry was an intermediate station on the joint line between Hooton and Birkenhead. It grew in importance in 1891 on completion of the Mersey Railway extension from Green Lane, allowing passengers to change from one system to the other, and a new station was opened. On 4 August 1966 2-6-4T No 42647 arrives from Birkenhead with a Chester service, while on the far side 9F 2-10-0 No 92070 heads north with a freight train. There was a through freight line leading to Birkenhead Docks and Bidston, which, although mostly in situ today, has not been used for a number of years.

In the 'present' picture Class 508 unit No 508104 enters the station with an Ellesmere Port service. These alternate with trains to Chester, offering a 15-minute-interval service as far as Hooton, then half-hourly to each destination. Half of the southbound platform has been fenced off and the freight line lies beyond on the far side of the station. *Dr L. A. Nixon/JCH*

4
4
4
4
M28377M
LIVERPOOL CENTRAL
M29143M
Trains
to Liverpool
3

4
4
4

Opposite ROCK FERRY (2): This photograph, dated 4 September 1982, shows the two bay platforms at the north end of the station occupied by Class 503 units, with cars M28377 and M29143 visible. Although the first 19 Class 503s were built for the Wirral electrification in 1938, the second batch of 24 units was not constructed until 1956, remaining in service until replaced by the arrival of the Class 508s on the Wirral in 1984/5 (the 507s having initially all gone to the other side of the river).

In an endeavour to discourage trespassers and vandals a fencing barrier has been erected, as seen in the picture taken on 9 January 2002. The flats and houses on the right remain in the background. *Gavin Morrison/JCH*

ROCK FERRY (3): A second view of the two bay platforms, this time taken from the north end of the station looking south. Two Class 503 units headed by cars M29147 and M29139 await their next turns of duty on 4 September 1982.

Comparison with the shot taken on 2 July 2002 shows that the central siding has been removed, but there is little change either to the station buildings on platforms 2/3 or to the buildings on the skyline. Class 508 No 508128 is about to leave from one of the through platforms. *Gavin Morrison/JCH*

Hooton to West Kirby

HADLOW ROAD was the first station beyond Hooton on the line to Parkgate. It opened in 1866 and had substantial brick station buildings and a passing loop. The picture was probably taken in the 1920s and shows a train entering the loop, with the signalman standing by the track to exchange the single-line token.

The station closed to passenger traffic in 1956, but the buildings have been beautifully preserved and are kept in immaculate condition by park rangers working for Cheshire County Council Countryside Management of Wirral Country Park, as can be seen in the photograph of 5 February 2002. However, things are not quite what they seem, as the signal box, while carrying the name Hadlow Road, is actually an ex-North Staffordshire Railway box displaced from Hassall Green, near Sandbach. The signal has been added at some point. Nonetheless the recreated scene attracts many visitors and is a great credit to those in charge. *John Ryan collection/JCH*

HESWALL was another intermediate station on the Hooton to West Kirby line, opened in 1886. In this Edwardian view the signalman steps out with the train staff for the single line to Parkgate. The approaching train en route to Hooton is formed of four-wheeled coaches and is hauled by an LNWR Webb tank engine. The spick and span look of the station is a pleasure to see.

After the station closed in 1956, and the line in 1962, the British Railways Board sold an 8-acre site for housing development, presumably before anyone had thought of preserving the whole line for the Wirral Way. Remarkably the station house remains and, in the view taken along Riverbank Close on 5 February 2002, it can be seen between the street lamp and telegraph pole. *Mike Hitches collection/JCH*

THURSTASTON station was opened in 1886 when the line from Parkgate was extended to West Kirby. The station consisted of two platforms, one of which was accommodated by a loop, as the line was single track. The 'past' picture was taken looking south, showing the loop line as well as the goods sidings off to the left, beyond the station.

Passenger traffic ceased when the station closed in 1954, although the line did not close until 1962. Today the site of the station has a visitor centre, being part of the Wirral Way Country Park, and it is a popular starting place to walk the old trackbed. Both platforms are still in situ. The 'present' picture, taken on 5 February 2002, shows the loop platform; note that the fir tree has retained most of its shape in the 50-odd years since the first picture was taken! *Stations UK/JCH*

KIRBY PARK was the last intermediate station on the Joint Line from Hooton to West Kirby. Opened in 1894, it closed to the public in 1954 but remained in use by pupils of the nearby Calday Grange Grammar School until 1956. It consisted of a simple platform and modest wooden building, with a coal siding that can be seen to the right in the picture taken on 7 August 1954 of ex-GWR 2-6-2T No 4124 with a three-coach train of ex-LMS stock from Hooton.

Today the trackbed is part of the Wirral Way, with no sign of the railway left at all, and only the road bridge providing a link with the past, as seen on 2 July 2002. *N. R. Knight/JCH*

WEST KIRBY (JOINT STATION): Opened as a terminal from Parkgate by the Birkenhead Joint Company in 1886, West Kirby became a through station when the connection was made with the Wirral Railway, just to the north, later in the same year. On 20 September 1954 ex-GWR 0-4-2T No 1457 has brought in the 2.50pm from Hooton, formed of auto-coach No 212, and is moving back to take water. Although the branch did not finally close until 1962, the through platforms at West Kirby closed in 1956.

In today's comparison, taken on 27 March 2002, the photographer is standing on the site of the old station. All traces have disappeared and the bridge has gone, but the Brookfield Road houses remain and the course of the line to Kirby Park can be seen to the right, now the entrance to the Wirral Way. *H. C. Casserley/JCH*

Birkenhead

BIRKENHEAD MOLLINGTON STREET LOCO SHED was situated on a short spur from the line to Woodside. It was opened in 1879 by the GWR and LNWR, each having an eight-road shed side by side. It was rebuilt by the LMS in the late 1930s, when the length was reduced and a new roof fitted, while the GWR shed was cut back and re-roofed in 1961 by BR London Midland Region. In 1947 the GWR allocation was 43 locos and the LMS 51. The shed closed to steam in 1967 but continued as a diesel depot until 1985, finally being demolished in 1987. Taken in 1982, the 'past' photo shows Class 40s, Mersey electric 503 units and a Class 25.

On 14 February 2002 the site of the shed remains undeveloped, while the gasometers and building belonging to the gas works remain.

The third photograph (*above*) shows the shed in steam days, with several BR 9F 2-10-0 freight engines 'on shed' together with ex-LMS 8Fs and an 'Austerity'. *Gavin Morrison/JCH/Tom Heavyside*

WOODSIDE was a fine spacious station that opened in 1878, situated close to the ferry terminal and within a few minutes walk of the town centre. The traffic prospered and shortly before the First World War it is recorded that well over 400,000 tickets were issued in one year. At its peak there were over 150 train movements a day, including those of empty stock. Paddington services would reverse and change engine at Chester and perhaps be taken on south by a 'County' or a 'Castle'. It had always been a dream of the GWR to reach Liverpool via Birkenhead, and for a short period at the end of the 19th century it ran through

coaches from Paddington via the river tunnel to Liverpool Central Low Level, but the problems were numerous and by 1900 the service had ceased. In the 'past' picture BR Standard 4MT 2-6-0 No 76020 is seen on 5 March 1966, the year before the station closed.

The site is currently used, rather ironically, as a parking area for Arriva buses. In the 'present' picture, taken on 14 February 2002, the retaining wall and bridge remain, together with several of the buildings beyond. *B. Taylor/JCH*

BIRKENHEAD CENTRAL (1): In this picture, of unknown date, two of the original Westinghouse electric units, which were painted green and lasted until 1956, pass each other, and to the right is the original carriage shed, later to be extended as additional rolling-stock was needed. The Railway Signal Company of Fazakerley supplied the signals and signalling equipment.

Comparison with the new picture taken on 9 January 2002 shows that the canopy on the left-hand platform has been cut back and the carriage shed extended. The footbridge was moved near to the Liverpool end of the platforms, as seen in the third picture, also dated 9 January 2002. A Class 507 is in the southbound platform and another unit is stabled by the side of the carriage shed, the latter appearing to be out of use. *E. C. Lloyd collection/JCH (2)*

BIRKENHEAD CENTRAL (2): The station and carriage shed are pictured in 1953. The Westinghouse stock was replaced by the Class 503 units in 1956, and they were followed by the 508s, which started to arrive on Wirral in October 1983. At that stage the 507s and 508s did not mix, being allocated to Northern (ie Southport, Ormskirk, etc) and Wirral lines respectively.

The carriage shed has been modified over the years and was completely empty when the 'present' picture was taken on 9 January 2002. The bay platform has gone, but platform canopies have appeared. A number of buildings beyond the depot in the older photograph have been demolished, enabling the skyline of Birkenhead to be seen more clearly. *Jim Peden collection/JCH*

HAMILTON SQUARE was opened in 1886, and this posed picture of the platform staff was taken looking towards the river tunnel around 1910. The lighting would have been by incandescent gas at that time and would have been rather dim. A sign on the left-hand side tells 1st Class passengers where to wait for their compartments on each train, which ran in fixed formations.

In contrast is the brightly lit station of today, photographed on 14 February 2002. The destination board shows three trains due for Liverpool Central within 11 minutes, as well as advising the number of cars on each service. And not a member of staff to be seen! *E. C. Lloyd collection/JCH*

BIRKENHEAD PARK: When the station was opened in 1888, it was rather curiously under the auspices of the Birkenhead Park Station Joint Committee, no doubt reflecting the connection between the Wirral Railway and the Mersey Railway. The two companies amalgamated in 1891 using the Wirral Railway name. On 19 October 1946 unit No 10 with 'Mersey Railway' on the side enters the station en route to Liverpool.

Consisting originally of two island platforms, in the early 1990s one platform was removed and the remaining one widened. At the same time the trackwork was simplified to one line in each direction, as can be seen in the 'present' picture dated 2 July 2002. The building beyond the station above the bridge was the first purpose-built community hall in the north of England, erected for the parishioners of Trinity Church. *H. C. Casserley/JCH*

BIDSTON SHED was built in 1897 by the Manchester, Sheffield & Lincolnshire Railway, which later became the Great Central Railway, then part of the LNER and finally British Railways (LMR). Situated on the south side of the Birkenhead to West Kirby line, close to Birkenhead North station, the shed consisted of a straight two-road building, originally with a 'northlight'-pattern roof, later re-roofed with a brick screen. In the view taken on 19 September 1959, looking east, we can see two ex-LMS 8F 2-8-0s, Nos 48253 and 48348, BR Standard 2-10-0 No 92047, and ex-LNER 0-6-0T J72 No 68671 on the right, all local engines at that time. The shed was very much freight-orientated and with the gradual run-down of freight activity on the Wirral it closed in 1963. Today nothing remains and the area has been completely redeveloped for industry and recreation, as seen on 5 March 2002.
H. C. Casserley/JCH

CANNING STREET NORTH: The tracks of the Mersey Docks & Harbour Board formed a through freight-only route between Rock Ferry and Birkenhead North. Their main use, however, was to provide access to the various sidings in Birkenhead Docks. On 6 July 1983 Class 25 No 25109 approaches Canning Street North with a local trip working from Birkenhead Cavendish sidings to Ellesmere Port. The train conveys mainly empty HTV hopper wagons from Birkenhead North coal depot. The headcode box on the locomotive displays the characteristic two spots of this era, following BR's decision in the mid-1970s to do away with headcodes. The HTV wagons were by now towards the end of their working lives and would soon be replaced by air-braked HEAs.

While the steps to the footbridge from which the 'past' picture was taken remain, the flooring has gone! The track is in situ, although heavily overgrown, the signal post has been shortened, and the sidings to the right have been removed, as photographed on 14 February 2002. *PDS/JCH*

DUKE STREET SWING BRIDGE: Perhaps the most interesting survival in the Docks system in the 1980s was this swing bridge at Duke Street, dividing the East from the West Float and providing shared rail and road access to the terminals on the north side of the water. The 1980s saw a brief revival of grain traffic to two terminals in Birkenhead Docks, and here Class 03 shunter No 03189 is propelling Polybulks carrying grain from Chettisham, near Ely, and Newmarket across the bridge on 6 July 1983, causing a temporary interruption in road traffic. The air-braked privately-owned Polybulks would have reached Birkenhead on the overnight wagonload Speedlink service from Whitemoor, an option not available for the vacuum-braked BR-owned CGV hopper wagons also in use at this time.

Despite their modern design and high capacity, the Polybulk wagons failed to stem the gradual loss of rail-borne grain traffic. Attempts to convey the business in full trainloads were unsuccessful because of the large number of terminals involved and the seasonal nature of many flows. Following the end of rail traffic across the swing bridge, the track was lifted, but the control cabin remains much the same and the bridge is still opened to allow ships to move between the West and East Floats. On 14 February 2002 an Arriva single-decker crosses the bridge en route to New Brighton. *PDS/JCH*

J. RANK SIDING: Shunter No 03189 is seen again propelling a rake of CGVs carrying grain from Chettisham into the J. Rank siding alongside the line to Birkenhead North on the afternoon of 6 July 1983; the sidings were situated on the south side of the West Float. No 03189 was one of three Class 03 shunters allocated to Birkenhead Mollington Street at this time for duties in and around the Docks.

Although today parts of the building remain, most of it has been demolished, and the area has been fenced off, as seen in the photograph dated 14 February 2002. The track has not been used since the last train went to the coal concentration depot, further along the line towards Bidston, in 1993. *PDS/JCH*

New Brighton and Seacombe branches

Opposite SEACOMBE was opened in 1895 by the Wirral Railway as Seacombe, became Seacombe & Egremont in 1901, then reverted to just Seacombe in 1953. The only other station on the branch, which was off the Birkenhead to New Brighton line, was Liscard & Poulton. There were direct services from Seacombe to the nearby resort of New Brighton until 1911, to West Kirby until 1938, and to Wrexham until closure of the Seacombe branch in 1960. On 17 November 1951 ex-LMS 2-6-2T No 40080 (allocated to 6E, the ex-GCR/LNER shed at Wrexham Rhos Ddu) is ready for the 11.28am departure, which will call at all 18 intermediate stations en route to Wrexham Central.

Today the area has been completely redeveloped and the only point of recognition is the tower of the ferry terminal, as seen in the 'present' picture taken on 5 March 2002. _Jim Peden/JCH_

This second view of the station shows ex-GCR 4-4-2T No 67412 arriving with the 9.35am from Wrexham on 10 August 1953, seven years before closure of the branch line in 1960. Engines of this class were allocated both to Chester Northgate and to Wrexham Rhos Ddu sheds. There is nothing left today to form a link with the railway, other than memories! _H. C. Casserley_

WALLASEY GROVE ROAD: The station, originally just Wallasey, dates back to 1888 when the line was opened by the Seacombe, Hoylake & Deeside Railway (later to be amalgamated into the Wirral Railway). The line was extended to New Brighton later in the same year. A smart-looking Wirral Railway 0-4-4T is seen approaching from New Brighton, with a consist of four-wheel carriages, probably shortly before the First World War. The line was electrified in 1938 and the station was renamed Wallasey Grove Road in 1948 to avoid confusion with Wallasey Village station.

On 15 January 2002, some 80 years later, the building shows remarkably little change: the mock Tudor chimneys have gone, as have the clock, the porter's trolley and no doubt the porter too, but the Wirral Horn remains on the front of the right-hand gable. *John Ryan collection/JCH*

NEW BRIGHTON (1): When the station was opened in 1888 by the Seacombe, Hoylake and Deeside Railway (later to become the Wirral Railway), the town of New Brighton was already a popular destination. This view, looking east, was probably taken around the turn of the last century. To the right of St James's Church spire is the famous tower, opened in 1900. A Wirral Railway tank engine is simmering in the station at the head of a short train destined for Birkenhead Park or the nearby resort of Seacombe. Ironically, one of the newly introduced tramcars can be seen in Victoria Road, which no doubt contributed to the demise of the branch line. The fence down the middle of the platform was erected to segregate arriving and departing passengers. From October 1923 to September 1939 the LMS ran through coaches to Euston via West Kirby and Hooton.

Today's view, taken on 27 February 2002, shows an industrial estate where the goods yard was once situated; the tower has gone but the church remains and the station building is not much altered, although a concrete canopy has been added over the platforms to offer some protection for passengers. Class 507 and 508 units occupy four of the five roads; the destination of all services now being Liverpool Central. *E. C. Lloyd collection/JCH*

NEW BRIGHTON (2): Another wonderful postcard view, franked in 1906. Looking west from the buffer stops, a smart-looking tank engine has just arrived with a rake of four-wheel coaches. The loco crew and porters pose for the photograph, while another porter pushes a basket, no doubt containing costumes for one of the town's theatres.

In the view on 15 January 2002, taken from underneath the added concrete canopy, most of the buildings on the left are hidden by the trees and there is no longer a goods yard on the right. Portland Street overbridge remains beyond the station. *John Ryan collection/JCH*

NEW BRIGHTON (3): Taken towards the end of the 19th century, this view of the station frontage shows the clock at 2.00pm, which was likely the shift change time, explaining the large number of staff posed for the picture – very different from today! Apart from the removal of the large sign and clock tower and the blocking out of the windows on the left-hand side, the building shows remarkably little alteration about 100 years later on 27 February 2002. *Stations UK/JCH*

Bidston to West Kirby

BIDSTON (1): East of the station was a triangular junction, which allowed freight such as imported iron ore from Bidston Dock to reach Dee Marsh and beyond via the ex-GCR/LNER line. Two Class 25s, Nos 25275 and 25165, are seen coming off the western leg of the triangle on 14 July 1976 with a train of imported iron ore from Bidston Dock to John Summers steel works at Shotton.

The iron ore trains continued to run until April 1980, when Shotton ceased making steel. Subsequently that side of the triangle was severed, and now serves only as a siding. Class 508 No 508112 is approaching Bidston station (behind the photographer) with a West Kirby service on 5 March 2002. As can be seen, there has been a remarkable change in the skyline, where the landscaping of a refuse tip has produced a completely new hill. *Tom Heavyside/JCH*

BIDSTON (2): On 19 September 1959 BR Standard 2-6-2T No 82020 stands in the station with the 2.40pm service from Wrexham to Seacombe. It will use the triangular junction east of the station to gain the New Brighton branch before taking the Seacombe line. The station was a true interchange enabling passengers from the Wrexham line to change for a direct train to Liverpool.

More than 40 years later the signal box has gone and the station lights have been substituted by a modern design, but the station building remains much the same. Class 508 No 508136 is ready to depart with a Liverpool to West Kirby service on 27 February 2002. *H. C. Casserley/JCH*

MORETON: The large Cadburys biscuit factory on the north side of the line just east of Moreton station was still rail-connected in the mid-1950s. Fuel was brought in, generally off the LNER line, which meant reversing at Bidston, while the biscuits travelled out in vans, some of which were branded 'Return to Cadburys Moreton, Wirral'. The Company had its own shunting loco, No 14, a Hudswell Clarke, which has been preserved outside the main entrance to the factory, as seen in the inset. On 4 August 1966 ex-LMS 'Crab' 2-6-0 No 42727 heads east after leaving the factory sidings; the 8H shedplate shows that the engine was allocated to Birkenhead (changed from 6C in 1963).

The rail connection was taken out of use by the early 1970s but the factory remains, shared with Typhoo Tea, as seen in the picture taken from the west end of Leasowe station on 27 February 2002, with Class 507 No 507030 approaching on a West Kirby to Liverpool service. *Dr L. A. Nixon/JCH*

MEOLS was the next station west of Moreton, and was rebuilt in the late 1930s in an almost 'art deco' style, as seen on 20 September 1959 in this east-facing view. The tall semaphore signals at the end of the platform enabled train drivers to see over the top of the road bridge as they approached the station. The distant is for Carr Lane crossing.

Today, apart from some minor changes to the platform building and the loss of the semaphores, the scene has hardly changed in the intervening 43 years. The later photograph was taken on 2 July 2002 and shows a Class 507 approaching with a West Kirby train. *H. C. Casserley/JCH*

HOYLAKE station was opened in 1866 by the Hoylake Railway. Due to disappointing traffic returns it closed four years later, but re-opened in 1872. In our 'past' picture, likely to have been taken in the late 1930s, a tank engine is seen entering the station at the head of a train bound possibly for Hooton via West Kirby, as an electric train is setting off towards Birkenhead. Electrification took place in 1937/8, when the station buildings were modernised.

The 'present' picture, taken on 15 January 2002, shows that the coal yard on the left-hand side has gone, as have the semaphore signals and the gasometer, but the station buildings show remarkably little change. A Class 507 approaches with a Liverpool to West Kirby service. *Stations UK/JCH*

THE STATION FROM THE BRIDGE
WEST KIRBY

WEST KIRBY

WEST KIRBY: The first station at West Kirby was opened in 1878 by the Hoylake & Birkenhead Rail & Tramway Company, later to become the Wirral Railway. The line prospered and the station was rebuilt in 1896. In the meantime, the Birkenhead Joint had opened its own terminus from Hooton in 1886, which subsequently became a through station, the two lines being joined by means of the connection that can be seen to the left of the picture. The Wirral line station consisted of a long platform with two faces, similar to New Brighton, with additional sidings for empty stock and goods; the concrete canopy was not installed until 1937. In the 'past' picture a tank engine stands with a train for Birkenhead on the right-hand side. Another engine is blowing off steam in the goods yard.

The second picture, taken on 27 March 1983, shows a line-up of Class 503s, with car No M28373 heading the 1137 to Liverpool Central. The original signal box has been replaced, the goods yard has gone, but some of the skyline buildings remain.

Today, as seen in the third picture, the station trackwork has been further simplified and the signal box has gone. All trains are now controlled from Sandhills on the other side of the Mersey. Class 508 No 508135 is seen leaving for Liverpool on 27 March 2002. *E. C. Lloyd collection/PDS/JCH*

Bidston to Shotton

UPTON was the first station south of Bidston on the line to Shotton and Wrexham, and opened in 1896. It once boasted a booking hall on the road bridge and well-built brick waiting shelters, as seen in the picture taken from a Wrexham-bound train on 10 August 1953. On the left is a local landmark in the form of a sandstone shaft, part of an old waterworks, that remains behind the trees.

The station has since undergone a total modernisation with only 'bus-stop'-type shelters remaining, as seen in the 'present' picture with Class 150 unit 150222 heading towards Bidston on 27 February 2002. Currently Upton is a request stop for all except two trains in each direction. *H. C. Casserley/JCH*

NESTON: Opened in 1896, the station underwent several name changes, first to Neston & Parkgate, then to Neston North (to avoid confusion with the other Neston station on the Hooton-West Kirby line) and finally back to Neston in 1968. Despite being above road level and having wooden platforms mounted on stilts, the station buildings were made of brick and were quite substantial. In our 'past' photograph, the nameboard 'Neston North' suggests a date between 1952 and 1968. The GCR-style Neston signal box, which remained until 1969, is at the far end of the station and almost opposite a water tower.

The station has recently been completely modernised and now just has two 'bus-stop'-type shelters. On 5 February 2002 Class 153 No 153359 departs for Bidston. All the units used on the line at the time of writing are based at Newton Heath depot in Manchester and are operated by First North Western. *Stations UK/JCH*

BURTON POINT: The line from Dee Marsh to Bidston was a joint venture by the Manchester, Sheffield & Lincolnshire Railway and the Wrexham, Mold & Connah's Quay Railway, formed in order to gain access to Birkenhead Docks. Named the North Wales & Liverpool Railway, the line was built in 1896, but Burton Point station was not opened until 1899. Despite its rather isolated position with few local inhabitants, the station buildings were quite substantial, made of yellow brick. Taken after the station closed in 1955, a BR 9F 2-10-0 passes through with loaded hoppers of iron ore en route from Bidston Ore Dock to John Summers steel works at Shotton.

Despite threats of closure the line has remained open, and in the 'present' photograph, dated 27 March 2002, Class 150 No 150149 heads south with a Bidston to Wrexham Central train; on weekdays there is an hourly service. One of the platform buildings has survived the nearly 50 years since closure, as has the nearby station house. *Keith Sanders/JCH*

SHOTTON HIGH LEVEL: Although located just on the Welsh side of the River Dee, Shotton High Level was a junction for two lines in England – the main route north to Bidston and Seacombe and the branch heading east to Chester. Opened in 1891 by the Wrexham Mold & Connah's Quay Railway as Connah's Quay & Shotton, it was renamed to the present title in 1953. Both lines retained their Great Central feel well into the British Railways era. On 10 August 1953 ex-Great Central Class C13 4-4-2T No 67412 is about to leave with the 3.45pm from Wrexham to Seacombe.

The signal box (Hawarden Bridge Junction) and signals are long gone and the track has been simplified, but the path to the lower-level station enabling interchange with services along the North Wales Coast is still there. Class 142 No 142033 enters the station with the 1432 from Bidston to Wrexham Central on 2 February 2002. *H. C. Casserley/PDS*

INDEX OF LOCATIONS